FERRETS AND FERRETING

FERRETS AND FERRETING

A PRACTICAL MANUAL ON THEIR BREEDING, MANAGING, TRAINING AND WORKING

With Chapters on Working and Shooting
By ARTHUR NIBLETT.

FIFTEENTH EDITION

THE BAZAAR, EXCHANGE & MART, LTD.
LINK HOUSE, 24, STORE STREET, LONDON, W.C.1.

Made and Printed in Great Britain by
St. Stephen's Bristol Press, Ltd., 1, Broadmead, Bristol 1.

CONTENTS

FERRETS AND FERRETING

CHAPTER I.

The Ferret and Its Allies.

OF the many notable and interesting animals which constitute the great natural history family of the *Mustelidæ*
not the least remarkable is the ferret. Though by some
authors accorded specific rank, and stated to be an introduction from Spain to Africa, yet in reality it is nothing
more than an albino (or practically so) domesticated
variety of the polecat. Indeed, the latter has been kept
in captivity and worked against rats after the manner of
ferrets. The so-called black ferret is nothing more than
a male polecat in his new coat. The ferret has for its
immediate congeners in the genus Mustela, the martins,
the polecat, the stoat, and the common weasel, whilst
allied to it are the otter, the badger, and the skunk. Of
the mustelines proper, what one says regarding the general
characteristics of form, habit, and nature of one, is more
or less true of all together. They all possess the same
low, elongated, lithe, muscular bodies; they are all
predatory, bloodthirsty, determined of purpose, and
relentless; they are constitutionally hardy, prolific, foul
of odour, yet withal of scrupulously clean habits; their

1

haunts vary only in having their peculiarities more or less
pronounced. Between the martens and the polecats and
weasels there is a great difference as regards the dentition.
The former have four pairs of pre-molars in each jaw;
the latter two have but three.

There is no need to enter into any lengthy description
of the ferret; its yellowish-white body, sharp, intelligent
aspect, and curious, pink eyes, are features which
have made it universally known. This is the common ferret; but there is also the polecat ferret, the
result of a cross between the two animals. The latter
partakes more of the outward aspect of the wild polecat,
whilst retaining the general nature of the ferret. As a
rule the cross is larger than the ordinary kind; but
curiously enough the smallest ferrets seen are usually also
of this variety. Opinions differ as to which is the better
sort of the two for work; but it is reasonable to suppose
that, on the whole, polecat ferrets are more agile in
pursuit than white ferrets, which points to their being
more suited to rats than to rabbits; whilst the colour of the
white ferret is a merit which should never be overlooked
in connection with rabbiting. In regard to hardiness,
breeding propensities, and such-like matters, there is not
much to choose between the two; both are more or less
difficult to rear, but better and healthier progeny are
obtained from a good strain of polecat ferrets than from
the white, though they require more careful handling.

Of the other congeners of the ferret, the weasel and
the stoat resemble one another in colouring and form,
but are more rat-like in many other respects, whilst
possessing the same very pronounced predatory instincts.

The ferret is undoubtedly, as stated elsewhere, but a

modified polecat, and it is therefore to some extent a matter for wonder that serious attempts are not oftener made to tame and domesticate this indigenous species, and utilise it as we do the ferret. The mere crossing of the two at times points to the very probable success of such an undertaking. The polecat has decreased at a rapid rate in the British Isles; and after all, it is both an interesting and beautiful creature, worthy of retention amongst the ranks of our furred animals; this retention would be greatly assisted were the suggestion here made carried into effect. The polecat is also known as a fitchet, fitch, fitchet-weasel, and foumart.

A curious trait, worthy of note here, is that the ferret never appears to run really foul of any of its congeners. There is always a sort of armed neutrality amongst them; they never seem to fight, but to steer clear of one another, and, when ferreting, one will often have this made apparent. Where stoats and weasels are plentiful, many failures with ferrets may be thus accounted for.

Many other points in connection with the natural history of the ferret will make themselves known as the practical parts of the subject-matter are reached; but without going further into them now, it may be laid down as a good axiom that success in breeding, training, and working ferrets is, in a great measure, dependent upon a proper appreciation of the importance of all that bears upon the habits of the animal, and a due recognition of the necessity of bowing to the lesson that every fact teaches.

CHAPTER II.

Ferret-Keeping—Hutches—Ferret Courts.

THOSE who "keep ferrets" are a numerous class of varied character, extending from the warrener, with his several dozen ferrets, to the suburban youth inclined to rural pursuits, with his ferret as a pet; between the two extremes are many descriptions of ferret-keepers, but to attempt to appeal in the limits of this little book to each and all of them would be beside the mark. We shall endeavour, however, so to shape our course as to hit off the happy medium, and to evolve a scheme which shall be generally applicable.

Ferrets are sometimes kept in large numbers: at others a few individuals comprise the stock. Taking the latter case first, when few are kept, then hutches will be found most suitable : whilst when any considerably quantity of them is needed a properly organised ferret court is found best to meet their requirements. In either instance one cardinal rule must always be observed—a fact that is made apparent by the nicety of habit of these creatures— namely, that the most scrupulous cleanliness must always be maintained, otherwise, without this and the necessary amount of warmth they also require, failure at first and disaster afterwards must surely accrue. Ferret-keeping should always be regarded as a serious matter, worthy of time and trouble being bestowed upon it; slipshod

4

dealings with these animals are always ill-advised and unpractical. Care and thoroughness always repay those who use them; and in connection with ferret-keeping, you cannot succeed unless you treat your stock in an intelligent and thorough manner.

The idea that an old box or other makeshift is good enough for ferrets is a mistaken one. To succeed with

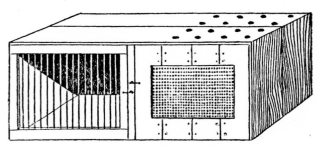

Fig. 4.—Ferret Hutch.

them you must provide a proper dwelling. A good hutch for them, say one or two, is that shown at Fig. 4, but provided with legs to keep it 2ft. or 3 ft. off the ground. The great thing is to give them a strongly-made, warm, dry, and sufficiently capacious and comfortable, well-ventilated hutch--and these qualities this one possesses. Many hutches described and recommended are too complicated in their construction, too dark, too small, or even too warm, for it is possible to err in this respect also. Where a number of ferrets are kept, several of these boxes will meet all the requirements of the case. It is better, if more than four ferrets have to be accommodated, to make a series of the hutches, rather than to enlarge the dimensions and only have one box.

Each hutch should measure 3ft. long 18in. high, and
18in. deep, and be divided into two equal compartments
by wood of the same thickness as the box is made of, viz.,
1in. board. The partition should have a round hole in
the centre, 4in. from the bottom. Some provision—either
a disc of wood or a small shutter—must be made to close
this aperture when needed. The sleeping-compartment
should be to the right hand, and be closed with a door of
wood having a space equal to half its surface cut out and
covered with the most finely perforated zinc, and fastening
to the centre partition—which projects to the level of
this door—by a small bolt. The door of the feeding-
compartment consists of a frame of wood 2in. wide, the
aperture being covered by small iron rods, or pieces of
stout wire, set longitudinally about ¾in. apart. The floor
of the hutch if of wood should have a number of holes
bored in it, in order to allow liquid to drain away. When
a series of these ferret dwellings is made it is better to
form the tops of the sleeping or breeding compartments,
as well as the inner sides, in the manner recommended
for the door of these latter. The hutches should each
stand on four strong wooden legs.

For the purposes of feeding, small, square, galvanised
iron dishes, 6in. by 4in., by 2in. deep, are very service-
able, or, better still, the rimmed heavy earthenware pots
used by rabbit and coney breeders, because the ferrets
cannot well upset them and so add to the dampness of
their dwelling. Most boxes become thoroughly saturated
with offensive moisture; this, however, may be obviated
to a large extent if each hutch is provided with a tray of
sand to which the ferrets can have access, but it must be
changed each day. To mitigate the evil, the bottom and

sides—the latter to 6in. high—must be painted with three coats of impermeable paint, the joints and cracks of the boxes being well puttied up so as to leave no small places where moisture and filth can accumulate. Portland cement and water, mixed so thinly that it can be painted on, is a good substitute for the first-named material. Then if the boxes are regularly and properly cleaned, and the bottoms are sprinkled over with a little sawdust or finely-rubbed peatmoss litter, your ferrets will always be sweet and healthy. In designing this hutch it has been taken for granted that the ferrets will be kept under cover and in sheltered situations; those who propose to keep them out of doors must provide some additional protection, more especially water-tight roofs. A slanting roof supported on four stout wooden legs with a wall as the back affords all the protection needed. This roof should be covered with felt and corrugated galvanised iron. It should project from the front and sides—about eighteen inches in front and twelve inches on each side.

One such hutch as has been figured will easily accommodate one or two ferrets; and when more are required it is better to keep a spare box in hand, so that on cleaning days, which are thrice a week, by changing the occupants regularly each hutch in turn will obtain three or four days' airing. Into the sleeping-compartment clean oat-straw or nice fresh hay with a slight sprinkling of peat-moss litter, should be placed for bedding, whilst a little insect or disinfecting powder dusted over the whole will tend to keep the stock free from pests. The feeding-compartment should also have a little peat-moss litter in it.

An admirable ready-made hutch is supplied by Messrs Spratt's Patent, Ltd.; it is illustrated at Fig. 5.

A correspondent sends particulars of a hutch (Fig. 6) which never requires cleaning. The bottom is of course wire netting of two thicknesses, and the front is of finer

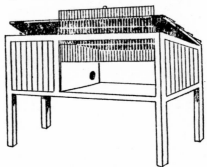

FIG. 5.—SPRATT'S PATENT FERRET-HUTCH.

netting. F is a tin made to fit in the door D. Two spare tins should be made to fit in F, and these should be changed every day. The empty one may be kept in a shed or even in the scullery and filled every morning. A is coarse

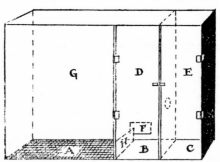

FIG. 6.—FERRET-HUTCH WITH WIRE NETTING BOTTOM.

netting, B and C are wood. There is no partition between G and D, except a small piece of wood H, which prevents the ferret from knocking food on the wire floor. A little sawdust should be placed on B, and hay in the sleeping-compartment C. D and E are wooden doors fastened by a button.

This form of hutch is most practical and one more suitable for persons who are pinched for room can be designed, and the trouble is almost nil. Once or twice in six months a little excrement may have to be removed from the wire bottom, but it can be got at from underneath, and is always dry and hard, and comes off clean. It is next to impossible for a ferret to contract foot-rot, and the air in the hutch never gets contaminated. Ferrets kept in such a house thrive and do well. If the wire in the bottom is too small in mesh, it does not allow the passage of excrement so well. A box containing sawdust might be fixed about 6in. below the bottom and independent of the hutch.

Though our correspondent recommends the use of wire bottoms, we cannot endorse his remarks. The fact is that foot-rot in the ferret is a specific form of mange due to the presence of a mite.

A good makeshift for one or two ferrets is an old potato-barrel. Knock out the ends, and join the three pieces which form one of them together, so as to present a smooth surface each side; then in each end of the barrel, 3in. from the extremity, nail some pieces of wood to project sufficiently to hold the circular end in its place when dropped into the barrel. For bedding use clean straw or hay. When you want to clean it out, invert the barrel—the ferret or ferrets having been previously removed—scrape the end, and set the barrel up again in a reversed position. In this way it will keep sweet and

dry for a very long time. A barrel does not make a bad
hospital for sick ferrets, and they are much cheaper, when
a number is required, than a similar quantity of regular
boxes.

The hutch should be hung against a wall, or be placed
on a trestle about 5ft. from the ground, and be so
disposed that the slope of the flooring is towards the back.

Where large numbers of ferrets are kept, besides the
breeding-hutches, a regular and well-organised ferret court
is advisable and even necessary. The mere keeping of
a great number of these animals in some enclosed place
will not suffice—they get wild and intractable; so that
one must really provide a properly-arranged court, some-
thing after the plan set forth in Fig. 7, which is drawn
to scale.

This court should be bricked or tiled, and the sides
should be of brick or wood, if within another builidng.
The measurements are shown on the plan.   The centre
division should be 3ft. high.   The partition—3ft. from
the inner end—is formed by a dividing board 1ft. high,
having six round holes 4in. in diameter cut in it, to face
the sleeping compartments, which are formed in similar
manner by boards 18in. high rounded off to the level of
the front.   The manner of fixing the dividing boards
between small strips of wood or runners, so that they can
be easily removed, is also shown. This admits of easy
and thorough cleaning.   The bedding in the sleeping-
compartments should be provided on the same lines as
recommended for the hutches, whilst the feeding-court
should have a portion of it covered with sawdust or peat-
moss litter, for the animals' convenience.

It will be seen that this court, large enough for fifty

ferrets, permits of the hobs being kept separate from the jills, whilst the division of the sleeping portion lessens the chance of disagreement. The ferrets, however, are bound to fight occasionally, in which case they are best left to settle their own grievances. The jills when in heat or with young must be removed to separate quarters in hutches; also, any sick or ailing ferrets must be similarly treated.

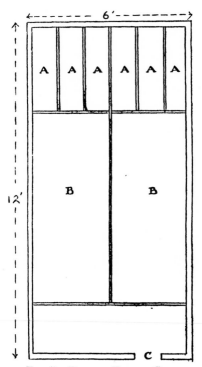

FIG. 7.—PLAN OF FERRET COURT.
a. a, a, Sleeping-Berths; *b, b,* Courts for Feeding and Exercise; *c,* Entrance to Court.

Mr. Lascelles Carr says :—" For some time past I have been keeping ferrets in hutches similar to those described in 'Ferrets and Ferreting,' but have found it almost impossible to keep them clean and healthy without bestowing an amount of trouble and attention upon the little animals which is not conveniently at my service. I have, therefore, with the aid of some suggestions made in the work already referred to, devised a method of keeping my ferrets, particulars of which, I think, may be of interest to every ferret-keeper.

" To begin, I may say it is necessary that one should have at disposal a small weather-proof building of some sort. I have appropriated to this purpose a part of a cowshed 9ft. in length by 6ft. deep, which I have fitted up as shown in the illustration (Fig. 8). The wooden

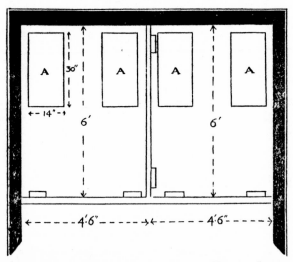

FIG. 8.—MR. LASCELLES CARR'S PLAN OF FERRET COURTS.

divisions are plain 1in. match-boarding, nailed together
with strips of the same material and arranged, as shown,
in two courts, the division-board being 3ft. high. These
form the courts for exercise; but as the ferrets require
warmer sleeping-places, I have placed in each court two
ordinary champagne-boxes (A, A) with loose lids, and with
a round 3in. hole cut at one end. Into these houses the
ferrets retire to sleep and to eat their food.

"I give them a little hay for a bed, which requires to
be changed not more than once a week, and then only for
the purpose of preventing it from becoming infested with
vermin. For the purpose of keeping these cubicles free
from damp, I have nailed two strips of wood underneath
the bottom of each. The floor of the exercise-court is
covered with moss-litter, and as the animals use one corner
for evacuating their excrement, I keep a bucketful of dry
ashes, and sprinkle a little of them over the evacuations.
Thus the place is always kept absolutely sweet and clean
with a minimum of labour."

A flooring composed of a mixture of cinders and tar,
making a kind of asphalt, has been recommended, but
such a floor is essentially bad, as it is absorbent and
therefore conducive to the propagation of those scourges
of the ferret-keeper—scours and foot-rot.

The court system as it is known, has much to recommend
it. Where there is any space at command a portion can
readily be enclosed by means of a few planks, and a
flooring of concrete or tiles laid down with a slight 'fall'
to facilitate washing down from time to time as necessary.
At the end of this enclosure should be placed a properly-
constructed hutch, raised slightly from the ground-level.
This is for sleeping in and for shelter during bad weather.

At other times the ferrets could exercise themselves in the fresh air. By nature they are active little animals, and it is a great mistake to keep them cooped up in small and often rudely-constructed unsanitary hutches, where neither sun or fresh air can penetrate."

CHAPTER III.

Feeding and General Management.

THE feeding of ferrets is a matter of considerable importance, because it has a great deal of influence upon the health and quality of the stock. There is no doubt that, as a rule, ferrets are both badly and unwisely fed; moreover, difference of opinion largely exists as to the proper time to feed ferrets when in work and when at rest.

From a fairly lengthly experience we have come to the conclusion that a flesh dietary is on the whole more suited to a carnivorous animal like the ferret than one in the main composed almost entirely of bread and milk. One would never think of giving such a dietary to a polecat kept in captivity. Why, therefore, advocate it for a ferret which, after all, is a modified polecat?

The foods we would suggest are those named hereunder : Freshly killed small birds; portions of rabbits containing the fur; heads and necks of poultry (but not the carcasses of such as have died from disease); rats that have been trapped where no poisons have been put down are also useful food. Again the livers from healthy poultry or indeed from ground game may be given, but the entrails of birds or other animals constitute an undesirable dietary.

Ferrets should be fed twice a day, allowing each individual to eat as much as it can without over-gorging, but taking care that no food is carried into the sleeping-apartment. The time for the chief meal is in the evening.

Mr. Lascelles Carr says:—" I entirely disagree with all the authorities I have read as to the ordinary methods of feeding. I give my ferrets *nothing* but animal-food, in the shape of fresh-killed birds, rats, or rabbits, or scraps of butcher's meat. This with a constant supply of fresh water is their only diet, and they appear to enjoy perfect health. They come to hand with the greatest freedom, are free from all ferocity, are always ready for work, and can work as long and as cleanly as any ferrets I have seen.

" I think one proof of the excellence of this method of diet is to be found in the fact that the evacuations of the animals have ceased to be foul and slimy, and have become dark and natural in appearance. I know how easy it is, and what a temptation exists, to dogmatise on matters of this sort."

The shooting and trapping expert of " *The Exchange and Mart* " shared Mr. Lascelles Carr's preference for a meat diet for ferrets. Replying to a correspondent of that paper, he wrote :—" It is a great mistake to feed ferrets upon an entirely bread-and-milk dietary. The ferret is a carnivorous animal, and in our opinion is never so healthy or so active as when subsisting chiefly upon a flesh dietary. We have tried both over a series of years, and we are convinced in our own mind which is the better food. Try both for a time with working ferrets, and note which gives the better results. When we feed our ferrets upon bread-and-milk we noticed that the fæcal discharges were always more or less watery and evil-smelling, and both adults and young (the latter more particularly) were subject to 'scours.' They were also far from active even though kept in roomy, well-ventilated, and scrupulously clean hutches. They, moreover, worked but in very half-hearted manner. No sooner, however, were they given a few freshly-killed birds or a few fowls' heads from the poulterer's, &c, than they underwent a change, and seldom were sick or sorry, and worked with the desired will and freedom.

"Some advocate a freshly-killed rabbit, preferably with the fur on; but others object to this on the score that the dietary is one calculated to make the ferrets, when used unmuzzled, kill instead of drive the rabbit out of a hole, and thus induce a wearisome 'lay-up.' When feeding, keep the ferrets so that the food is not taken into the sleeping-place to be devoured. That is where the court system comes in, as the ferrets soon learn to respond to the call, and the food may be given as a rule outside, or so fixed that it cannot be bodily taken therein. At any rate, hutches should be so constructed that the sleeping-place is shut off from the other portions."

As confirmatory of what has been said by Mr. Lascelles Carr and the expert of " *The Exchange and Mart* " upon the subject of feeding, we give the following interesting letter sent by a correspondent to that journal :—

There was a discussion in the columns of your valuable paper as to the best method of feeding ferrets. I have tried feeding my ferrets on a *flesh* diet alone with good results.

My ferrets are quite as tame as when fed on bread-and-milk; the chief differences I note are : (1) Their coats have grown rather longer and thicker, and the white ferrets have grown rather darker (possibly winter coats). (2) Their activity and muscular strength have been *greatly increased*. (3) They are cleaner and drier in their habits, and have lost all suspicion of " droop " and weakness about the hind legs, which I have often noticed in ferrets fed with bread-and-milk, being probably due to its action on the bowels.

On the whole, therefore, I have come to the conclusion that a
meat diet, with water (and occasionally milk) to drink, is the
best for ferrets.

Whatever the food given, it should always be
scrupulously clean and sweet; the feeding-tins should be
washed daily and be removed as soon as the ferrets
have eaten sufficiently. The quantity day by day per head
should never vary; the hours of feeding must be regular;
and the little creatures should always have their fill and
eat all that is given them, but not be allowed to gorge
to repletion.

The chief point where opinions amongst ferret-keepers
diverge is in connection with the feeding of ferrets which
are being more or less regularly worked. Whether not to
feed, to half feed, or to wholly feed them before working,
is a very vexed question. It seems most rational to treat
them quite in the ordinary way; and we fancy that, as a
rule, those who do so will find their ferrets work very well.
Both the other plans have great disadvantages; if you do
not feed your ferrets they will be too quick and sure to lie
up if they catch a rabbit; whilst if you only half feed
them they will tire out in half the time. It must be
admitted that ferrets fed immediately before being worked
will not prove at first as keen on their game as they might;
but they soon warm to their work. The most practical
plan to pursue is to feed your ferrets as usual, but an
hour at least before they are wanted; they will come up
to the scratch—in more senses than one—quite readily,
and, given a little food and an hour's rest during the
day, will work eight hours without losing much of their
dash and keenness.

Ferrets are thirsty little animals, and if you are going
out for a long day's ferreting some milk should be carried

so that they may have a drink now and again. When very thirsty they often go a long way to water; and many ferrets have been lost in underground drains with which the rabbit burrows have connected, when seeking for water to slake their thirst.

Ferrets like warmth, although indifferent to cold when in pursuit; and dryness is a necessity for them.

Many people keep their ferrets in a dark place; this is not wise. They cannot stand bright sunshine, but they like a moderately light dwelling. Light and air are essentials. Wild polecats kept in captivity are very liable to go blind.

CHAPTER IV.

Breeding Ferrets—Crossing.

BREEDING ferrets is a branch of our subject which requires, for the commanding of success, a larger amount of practical knowledge than any other. One may stumble along experiencing failure after failure, unaware where the weak link of the chain lies, and then suddenly jump into success. It is, and always will be, a business of some nicety. Ferrets are curious animals, and it is only when one arrives at a proper appreciation of their nature and habits that one is able to gauge the measure of their requirements and dislikes. More failures may be credited, we fancy, to over care than to lack of attention; but to both of these very fertile causes the great bulk of want of success may be ascribed.

The principles of ferret-breeding are fairly simple, but they should be followed. One does not breed promiscuously from dogs or poultry, and there is no reason why a haphazard line of operations should be adopted with ferrets. Two objects must always guide the breeder: one to produce a healthy strain; the other to produce a ferret of proper size and shape. For both rats and rabbits, medium-sized ferrets are the best; the idea of breeding small ones for rats and large ones for the rabbits is a wrong one. It stands to reason that small ferrets cannot do their work so well as medium ones, whilst large specimens are, as a rule, slow and lumbering; although

20

we must admit we have had one or two excellent big ferrets. Polecat ferrets are usually the largest, and we do not believe in the supposed merit of the first cross between the ferret and the polecat. We would employ the latter as a recuperative influence in a deteriorating strain, but that is all.

A good ferret should exemplify the type of the mustelines. A sharp muzzle; long, lithe, but withal muscular body, set on clean, muscular legs; and a good sweep in the turn of the animal's form are the main points of excellence. Blunt-headed, thickly-set ferrets are of wrong type and useless of purpose, and should never be used for breeding. Ferrets must be strong, active, healthy, hardy; so you must breed from individuals possessing these merits. Never breed from sickly or weak parents, nor from bad workers; but bear in mind that *pronounced* characteristics, whether bad or good, in the parents are repeated in the progeny in usually increased extent. Always try to breed from parents of a strain of good repute and good pedigree; make your own crosses, and watch their effects. When your strain shows evidence of diminishing excellence, raise it again by importing new blood; but, above all, breed up to a strain. of ferrets with great care and judgment, not promiscuously. If you have both white and polecat ferrets, breed them separately.

These, then, are the principles of ferret-breeding. No doubt if only numbers be the aim in view most of them may be abjured; but if high quality of your stock be desired—and this is what every practical man requires— then the principles of breeding must be observed.

The period of gestation of the ferret is, roughly speaking, six weeks, and the young—averaging six to ten in

number—are ready for working when four months old.
As in the case of the polecat, they are born in the spring
from May to July. The jill may be worked up to within
a fortnight of her time if it be necessary, and, in any case,
she should have plenty of exercise and food. When in
season, the female, or jill, should be placed with the male,
or hob, on two occasions, on alternate days, but otherwise
the sexes should be kept apart. When five weeks of her
time are up she must be placed in a clean, warm box, and
plenty of fresh litter be put in the breeding-compartment,
which should then be closed for six weeks. No observa-
tion or disturbance of it should be made until the young
are four or five weeks old, otherwise the jill may settle
the lot, and possibly savage the disturber.

After the age stated is reached they may be looked at
and counted during the time the dam is feeding, and some
fresh litter be supplied, the old to remain untouched. In
the meantime, there is no necessity to suspend the tri-
weekly cleaning of the other compartment, which must be
done directly the jill has finished feeding and has returned
to her progeny; the aperture between the two compartments is then closed, and the feeding portion of the
domain can be thoroughly dealt with. Ferrets with young
require feeding twice a day, and although a little warm
bread-and-milk may be given occasionally, flesh food
forms the usual dietary for these animals. After the
morning meal, and the possible cleaning out has been
accomplished, remove the remains of any food, and place
a small but heavy feeding dish of plain milk for the
dam, in case of her requiring it during the day.

At six weeks old the young see and commence to find
their way about, and at two months will come out and

feed with their mother, taking their full share of the food.
This is the most critical time of their lives, and for a
month on, from the time they see, young ferrets run the
risk of those ailments to which juvenile musteline nature
is heir. Distemper—sweat, or sweating ill, it is also
called—is the worst, and it sometimes causes decimation
in their ranks. When they reach two-and-a-half months
old the youngsters are weaned, and each brood is put into
a separate hutch, to remain there a fortnight, waiting
for any possible outbreak of distemper. All this time
they must be fed three or four times a day, be kept scrupulously clean, and any weaklings be removed and tended
separately; because it is usually the weak members of
the litters which first sicken, and the mere presence of a
sickly subject tends to lower the tone of the rest of the
litter and render them an easier prey to the fell malady.
At three months old they may be considered out of danger
and be removed to the ferret court, or be separated into
suitable batches.

Young ferrets should be handled from the earliest
possible moment, and by the time they have reached
twelve weeks of age it should be made a daily practice to
take them out and accustom them to being carried short
distances, being picked up and replaced upon the ground,
and transferred from one hand to another. At feeding-
time a regular call should be repeated; personally, it
always has been " Bun, Bun, Bun," uttered quickly in
one tone. Any ferret which shows decided signs of
intractability should be discarded, as the others are likely
to be influenced by it.

On the subject of handling, a breeder of long
experience says :—" Young unentered ferrets should be

handled when they are about three-parts grown, or a little
earlier perhaps." He adds the caution that as " ferrets,
like rabbits, some dogs, and many other animals, resent
a too early interference with their young, by destroying
them, care should be taken not to begin handling too
early. The ferrets should be handled round the neck, and
there must not be the slightest hesitancy on the part of the
handler, or the reward for his timidity—usually shown
by a quick withdrawal of the hand—will be a bite that he
is not likely to forget. Ferrets should from the first,
however, be accustomed to the owner, and should come
to his call. This may be readily done at feeding-time by
always using the same call or whistle." In the chapter on
" Working Ferrets for Shooting," by Mr. Arthur Niblett,
some useful observations on " handling " will be found.

In connection with the crossing of ferrets a few
remarks may be made. Breed between a dog polecat
ferret and a white jill; and if you want half strains of
polecat ferrets, breed between one possessing marked
features of the fitch or polecat type and a white one
sooner than between two crossbred fitch ferrets. If you
try to breed from a true polecat, it is better to cross it
with a white ferret than with one of the dark breed; the
progeny will be far easier to rear and train than were the
cross made between the real article and the semi-polecat.

Finally, it may be noted that ferrets live about five or
six years, but it is well known among breeders that they
will not live for long if not allowed to breed. This
applies to both sexes. A doe ferret will sometimes die
the first time she comes in season if she is refused access
to the buck.

CHAPTER V.

Training and Working Ferrets to Rabbits and Rats.

THE initial stages of training young ferrets, whether for rabbits or rats, are the same, so that until we come to the actual working of ferrets to rats it will suffice to refer solely to rabbits, regarding these as the quarry in either case.

We do not believe in beginning on artificial lines, by running a ferret through a pipe to a rabbit, as has been recommended by some writers; the idea is a farce. As soon as the young ferrets have become thoroughly accustomed to being handled, and are tame to the catch, they may be taken out to some small burrows. Everyone knows some " bury " or other, of small extent, where a rabbit is a sure find; and to the aforesaid bury the owner or keeper should go with one or two young ferrets. The old jill of the brood must be taken as well. The latter should be at first worked with a string and allowed into the burrow only a little way, two youngsters being put down with her. She will gradually entice them into the hole, and as soon as they show a disposition to follow her the line may be cast off, and the ferrets left to their own instinct. If a rabbit is found and moved by the mother, the young ones will soon be after it, and the probabilities are they will catch it and kill it. If so, all the better, even though they have to be dug out. It is first blood for them, and they will have learnt more in one such lesson than in a week's running through drain-pipes, and such-like procedure. Having got the ferrets out, take them next to a " play-hole," if you know of one, where you may reasonably expect there are *no* rabbits, but where rabbits have lately been. The more numerous the exits and elaborate the burrow—as a play-hole*—the better. Into this the two young ferrets should be let go. At first they may demur, but with a little coaxing they will soon start off and thoroughly ransack the burrow, and come out again. Should they come out at a hole, do not put them back at that hole, but at the original place of entry; they will know where they failed before, and try else-where, and it will teach them to come right out. If you always put your ferrets back into the holes where they show themselves, they will, in course of time, become shy and difficult to catch. Of course, these instructions hold good only when training ferrets; when they have become good workers you deal with the ferret as you consider most advisable in each individual case. When the youngsters have thoroughly run through this burrow they may be taken and tried at another; and then a trial may be made in earnest at some hole where it is reasonable to suppose a rabbit may be located. This form of training may be repeated daily until you consider your ferret ready for serious work. All the time, of course, the animal is being taught to come to hand easily, not to play about the mouths of the holes, and, as far as possible, not to

---

* A play-hole, in rabbiting parlance, is a burrow to which rabbits resort to play and to lie in during the day. Rabbits haunting plantations and low, scrubby coverts usually have their play-holes.

"lie-up." One should never hesitate to commence digging out a ferret that does not show itself quickly; we believe they learn a good deal from this. When training young ferrets to rabbits, they should never be allowed to lie-up more than ten minutes.

When teaching young ferrets you should net your rabbits at the holes, not shoot them. Then, when the rabbit bolts before the ferret, you can catch the former, and when the latter appears at the hole's mouth let it worry the rabbit an instant or two. Of course, the rabbit must be killed first; no one who possesses the smallest tinge of humane feelings would wilfully submit the rabbit to needless cruelty. One can be both a humane person and a sportsman at the same time.

As far as the training of ferrets to rats goes, but little can be said. The two animals are natural enemies and will attack one another; but you cannot put an inexperienced and immature ferret in to a rat and expect anything but the death or severe mauling of the former. Nor is there any reason why a rabbiting ferret should not be employed equally successfully for rats. A ferret that has never had anything to do with rats will benefit from being allowed to fight and kill a rat; and the young ferret should be turned down with the dam in a loose box or room, and a half-grown rat put down to it. This will be killed, probably by the jill, and after the young ferret has mouthed it about for a bit, the ferret should be taken up.

Some who have had considerable experience with ferrets disapprove of this plan on the grounds that ferrets, before being put to rats, require to be "blooded." The best way to do this is to kill a rat, and then place some of the

blood upon a live one, which is to be introduced to the
ferret, which will then make short work of it.

There are three ways of working ferrets when rabbiting : With a line, muzzled, or without a line or muzzle.
The first-named way is both ineffectual and unpractical ;
the second should be had recourse to only when necessary ;
and the last is the way in which everyone who uses
ferrets should endeavour to employ them.

FIG. 9.—LEATHER MUZZLE.

Of actual specially-constructed muzzles we have a poor
opinion, chiefly for the reason set forth below, but also
because they seriously hamper the ferret in its working
and, undoubtedly, materially handicap it.   The ferret is
a small creature, and if you put a leather muzzle weighing
2oz. on its head, you cannot but expect the animal to tire
much sooner than would otherwise be the case.   The
ordinary ferret-muzzle is made of thin, narrow little slips
of leather, much like an old-fashioned dog-muzzle.   One
loop goes over the snout of the ferret, two pieces reach
above and below to a second band, which passes round
behind the jaws of the ferret, and is fastened with a little
buckle, as shown in Fig. 9.   For working purposes these
muzzles are of very little utility, but when a ferret gets
sick and requires to be muzzled, they are the best to use.
We have seen the leather substituted by indiarubber, the

larger loop being stretched to get it over the head; and though effective enough in one way, they soon stretch and wear out, and, moreover, they mean starvation to a lost ferret.

One of the most complete muzzles consists of a small brass ring and screw-rod. The ring is passed over the snout of the ferret, and the rod behind the animal's canine teeth keeps it in place. The rod is shown as passing through, with a margin each side, but as a matter of fact, the head lies close to the ring, and the screw fits into a corresponding hole in the ring. There has been an improved muzzle of this description invented, where, by means of an ingenious arrangement, the one bar is done away with, and two smaller ones, working with a spring, are closed with a snap by pressure of the finger and thumb on either side. But with all such arrangements we find the same serious fault, and that is that in the event of the ferret being lost it must die a lingering and dreadful death of starvation, to the risk of which we do not consider anyone is justified in exposing it; whilst there is no doubt that such appurtenances greatly handicap the ferret when after rabbits. If the ferret is not to be sufficiently relied on, then it should be coped, but, as stated before, never muzzled. It is only ferrets that are too quick in running into their rabbit that require coping. To a large extent the question of killing and lying-up to a rabbit has nothing to do with it, because if a coped ferret catches a rabbit it will, in all probability, lie-up to it much longer and more persistently than would be the case were its powers of killing unrestricted. *A coped ferret cannot hold a rabbit* unless the latter lies in a blind alley; but in this case the ferret will scratch and worry at the rabbit sometimes for

hours, whereas if it were free it would kill the rabbit,
take a meal off it, and be on the move again. For these
and the previously set forth weighty reasons, we prefer to
work ferrets uncoped, certainly unmuzzled; but if they be
coped, it can be done in a thoroughly efficient fashion, and
in a manner of such temporary fashion that at the most it
would remain but forty-eight hours on a straying ferret.

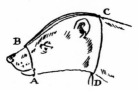

FIG. 10.—HEAD OF FERRET WITH COPE ADJUSTED.

We have made a sketch (Fig. 10) of a ferret's head,
showing the cope adjusted. The latter we have drawn
away from the head, so as to make it more apparent; but
when adjusted it would be as tight to the head as would
be reasonable. It is formed in the following manner :
Take a piece of whipcord about 12in. long, and unravel
it; then take one of the strands, and while you, or your
companion—most ferreters can cope their own ferrets—
hold the ferret, make a simple loop in the centre of it,
and place this over the bottom jaw of the animal just
behind the first canines. By pressing the jaws in a
backward direction, from top to bottom, you make the
ferret open them. Knot the loop below the jaw (A); then,
after pulling this reasonably tight—beneath the ferret's
tongue, by the way—take the two ends round, tie them
in a reefer's knot above the nose (B), measure them back
to just behind the line of the back of the skull (C), tie

them together again, and finally fasten them in a loop
beneath the throat (D), tight enough to prevent slipping,
but loose enough to allow free breathing-room for the
ferret. To make this quite clear here is a little projection
(Fig. 11) of the cope when knotted on to the animal.
This is a better plan than that of again joining the points
A and B in Fig. 10, because, in the latter case, it is easier

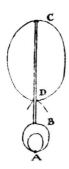

FIG. 11.—DIAGRAM OF FERRET-COPE.

for the ferret to catch its feet in the cope, when scratching at it to get it off. We have on many occasions lost
ferrets with this form of muzzle upon them, but they
have always turned up again well and evidently not
starved, with the nose-piece worn through, so that there
is no fear of their starving when lost.

At Figs. 12 and 13 another form of cope is shown;
but inasmuch as the points B and A in Fig. 12 are joined,
thus giving the ferret the hold necessary to enable it to
tear the muzzle off, we cannot recommend it against the
simpler form shown at Fig. 12, although some people
prefer to adopt it.

Upon the question of bells for ferrets, surely no two
opinions can lie—they are the best left alone. Any benefit
they may possess in the way of signalling the whereabouts
of a lying-up ferret is fully counterbalanced by their
many disadvantages. We believe in letting ferrets work
under natural conditions as far as possible.

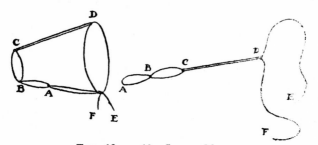

FIGS. 12 AND 13.—STRING MUZZLE.
B, C. D, Knots; E. F, Ends for tying under Throat, and
afterwards passing through Loop B A, to keep Jaw Band,
B C, in place.

The method of working ferrets on a line is somewhat
largely practised, considering its inefficacy. To the ferret
a thin, strong line is attached, and according as it works
so the line is run out or hauled in. The use of it, of
course, handicaps the ferret severely—it reduces its
chance of bolting any rabbits about 25 per cent.; the line
catches, or the ferret doubles on itself, nearly every time;
and, to cut a long story short, it is quite unpractical, and
only possible, with any measure of success, in small
burrows in a very sandy, clean, dry soil. Occasionally,
when one ferret lies up, you may move it by running in
another on a line, but beyond this we do not see where
the merits of the practice lie.

Upon the general working of ferrets there is no use in enlarging—the successful working of them can only be gained by experience; but some of the points of ferret-working may be referred to with advantage. When trying for rabbits, silence is of immense help; noise from talking, heavy walking, and such like, the scratching of your dog at the holes, all combine to handicap the ferret, by making the rabbit obstinate. Always put your ferret in at the lowest windward hole of the burrow. Ferret up a hedge and up wind. Use as few ferrets as possible, and persevere at each burrow. Never be rough in handling or attending your ferrets, keep them warm and dry, and work them considerately—coaxing rather than driving them, exciting sooner than pressing them.

When ferrets "lie-up," it is a case of the devil to pay. You cannot prevent it, but you can always reduce the frequency of such unpleasant occurrences by discarding any but good ferrets. . It is obviously natural that when a ferret catches a rabbit it should kill and make a meal off it; but it is unreasonable that it should make a point of doing this directly it is put in a burrow, and then go to sleep on the body of the victim. Some ferrets are prone to do this, and will incite others to do it; whilst, on the other hand, some reasonably fast ferrets will be so brisk upon their quarry that the rabbit has no chance but to bolt. Very slow and very fast ferrets are the worst offenders in this direction; the one of medium activity is usually less disposed to offend.

There are numerous remedies recommended and proposed for bringing out ferrets that are lying-up. The paunch of a newly-killed rabbit, placed in one of the windward entrances to the burrow, will sometimes fetch

the idler out; but the best means we know of is the
following preparation. Take some strips of rough, thick,
brown paper cut in lengths of 12in. by 2in. wide. Then
pound together in a mortar twelve parts of nitre and one
of cayenne pepper, and work this up into a thick solution
in water. Lay two slips of the paper on a board, paint
them with the solution, place one upon the other, and
repeat the process till six are similarly treated; roll them
up, dry them, and keep them in a tin box for future use.
When required, unroll one slip and re-roll it, place it as
far as possible in the most windward hole of the burrow,
and having lighted it, close the mouth of the hole, with
a sod of turf. If the fumes reach your ferret it will come
out within a few seconds. This is the best ferret-evictor
we know of. An " old hand " of our acquaintance gave
as an infallible recipe for lying-up the tying of a piece of
thin cord rather tightly round the tail.

When you have to dig out your ferrets, instead of
following the direction of the hole, use a well-wrought
iron—or, better, a steel—rod, 5ft. or 6ft. long, and with
one end pointed. By striking this sharply, like a spear,
into the ground, and placing the ear to its end, the sound
of the rabbit scratching will be distinctly conveyed, and
with a little care and intelligent use will soon be able
to hit off, within a few inches, the exact spot where the
ferret and rabbit are; and, by digging directly down-
wards, you will come upon them, and probably secure
both. Such a rod as this weighs very little, and is a
useful thing to carry when ferreting.

When rats are the quarry, always use a strong force
of ferrets, for rats are fierce, plucky fighters, and you
require to have your ferrets numerous enough to drive
the rats before them.

Ferreting rats out from buildings, and killing them
with dogs, etc., unless properly carried out in a determined manner, is a very uncertain mode, and its only use
is to bustle the vermin about and make them scared; but
on the other hand, if the work be done thoroughly, then
it rarely fails to leave its mark. In order, then, to make
the business productive of beneficial results, a systematic
raid must be arranged and carried out. Of course, the
chief thing is to have a good lot of ferrets well up to their
work, and at the same time large and strong enough to
show to good account in the many fights in which they will
have to engage. One should have a number of ferrets,
according to the extent of ground they will have to spread
over, and it is best to obtain about twice as many as one
wants to keep going at a time. One can thus, at intervals,
pick up any apparently becoming lazy, and substitute the
same number of fresh ones, eager to commence work
themselves and enliven the rest. There must also be a
fair sprinkling of dogs, but not too many, nor any other
than those which are really steady to their work and not
unduly excitable; for nothing is worse and more injurious
to any chance of effecting good results than a cur running
hither and thither without doing more than yelp and
distract the other dogs' attention. A good number of
people should be got together, and a plentiful supply of
means wherewith to kill any escaping rats; nothing is
better, in our opinion, than a good flat shovel for this
purpose. If any outlying exits of drains in any way
connected with the parts being ferreted exist, they should
be provided with wire eel-traps, which are sometimes used
as rat-traps in ordinary circumstances, but are of little
avail; however, when properly fixed under the conditions

named they often catch a good many. One must be careful to look at them continually, otherwise a ferret might get in, and, if among five or six rats, would have rather a rough time of it. In order to make this wholesale ferreting about the buildings a success an entire day should be devoted to it, commencing early in the morning; and, as it will probably take place in autumn or winter, it is necessary to take up the ferrets at from two to three o'clock. Corn-ricks, when rats unluckily have taken up their abode therein and are devastating them, should be immediately cleared out by ferrets, and every possible means of access to rats stopped. If ricks be built simply on the ground, then constant trapping and ferreting are the only means to alleviate or put a stop to the mischief.

When it is desirable to extirpate rats which have adopted a hedge for their abode, they can, if the holes of entrance and egress be discovered, be trapped by using a small-sized gin at each hole. Or, on the other hand, ferreting can, in such cases, be resorted to with beneficial results, two or three good dogs and active ferrets being necessary. We need, however, scarcely enter into any details as to how to proceed, either in this instance or when the rats are by the waterside, whether of ponds, ditches, or streams.

If a ferret is lost and has to be left out all night, the holes of the burrow should be well stopped up, and a little straw or hay placed in the mouth of one of them. Early the following morning the lost ferret will probably be found asleep in the hay or straw. We say early, for if left too long the ferret will get hungry and set off on its travels in search of food. A wire rat-trap, on the same principle as the common wooden mouse-trap, is useful for recovering a ferret; it should be set close to the mouth of the hole, all the others communicating with the burrow the ferret is in being stopped up. The bait should be the head of a rabbit, and a little straw should be placed at

FIG. 14.—BOX FOR CARRYING FERRETS.

the far end of the trap for the ferret to lie on in case it is caught.

With regard to carrying the ferrets when taking them to the scene of the sport, there is nothing like a small box with a handle (Fig. 14). This may be procured from Messrs. Boulton and Paul, who, with Spratt's Patent, are the chief caterers for the requirements of ferret-keepers.

CHAPTER VI.

Working Ferrets for Shooting.

By ARTHUR NIBLETT.

HOW well I remember ferreting in my school-boy days. It was always considered necessary to give the keeper forty-eight hours' notice in order that the ferrets might be starved. On the eventful morning Velveteens arrived, his side pockets bulged out with his ferret bags, for he always seemed ashamed to be seen carrying them. On our arrival at the first earth two ferrets were taken out of the bag, and the barbarous process of stitching up their mouths was commenced. They were then put in, but, no matter what size the earth, never more than two were used. If they did show up, Velveteens immediately fell on the top of them, remarking, "that's a lucky job!" and we went on to the next earth to repeat the same process. In this way, in a long and successful day, we sometimes got ten couple of rabbits.

I will now endeavour to explain the system adopted by a Scotch keeper—alas, no more—the very best man with ferrets I have ever seen. He and I, without any assistance, thought it a very poor day if we could not kill twenty-five couple of rabbits, and have even killed thirty-five couple, beginning about 10.15 a.m. on a December day, and stopping when daylight failed.

To manage a day such as this, your ferrets must be both thoroughly handled and bold, and you must have plenty of them. If your ferrets are bad to handle and shy, you will waste most of your time in catching them.

It is easy to have well-handled ferrets if you begin with them when quite young, and are always fiddling about with them. It is not easy, however, to get really bold ones. The secret of this is never to carelessly and closely in-breed, and never to breed from shy ones. Dogs and other animals that are not carefully in-bred are invariably shy and nervous, and it is the same with ferrets. There is nothing more annoying than to have ferrets shrinking away from your hand when you stoop to pick them up, and nothing more detrimental to making a big bag.

If it should be your misfortune to have one of this description, it is a very good plan to collar him, and to attach to the collar a bootlace, by which means you can get hold of him when he shies away from you. A bootlace is better than string, which gets wet, then kinks, and then gets round a root, and " there you are," and there you will probably remain till dark. A bootlace is free from all these faults, does not rot, and is just the right length. It is also very useful in another way, as you can, by it, hold a loose ferret under your foot, and thus have your hands free to shoot.

Young ferrets are better than old; they are quicker and keener. Big ferrets are also, to my mind, better than small ones for bolting rabbits. They have more forcing power, and rabbits on a non-bolting day want a lot of forcing. For this reason a ferret with good strong claws is advisable, for claws, as well as teeth, are elements

of persuasion. White ferrets are better than brown, as
they are more easily seen, otherwise the point is not worthy
of consideration in view of the fact that both the white
and the polecat coloured animal have a common origin.

If you want to make a big bag do not muzzle your
ferrets. Unless you have a savage one it is quite unnecessary, for well-fed ferrets seldom lie up for long, whereas,
on the other hand, muzzled ones will often lie up an
unconscionable time with a live, sulky, non-bolting rabbit,
necessitating your digging; and when you have got to
them the rabbit will bolt, going away not shot at, guns
having been laid aside. If an unmuzzled ferret had been
used, you would at least have had the consolation, after
your dig, of adding one to the bag, for the ferret would
have killed him. If you have to muzzle them do so with
string. Leather and brass muzzles are undesirable.

Have plenty of ferrets, and do not be afraid to use
them. If you come to a big earth which you think
contains ten or twelve rabbits, and has as many or more
outlets, put in four ferrets to begin with, and if they do
not move them put in two more. The old-fashioned plan
of putting in one or two ferrets into a big place is absurd.
Anyone who has dug after a lost ferret in the many
ramifications of a big bury will see at once how easy it
is for rabbits to dodge about and evade a single ferret
without bolting. And again, it is just as easy, if you
have to dig, to dig after four ferrets as after one, and
they are nearly certain to be all congregated together
round one dead rabbit. To add a further argument in
favour of my plea of using plenty of ferrets, I consider
that the more you use the less liable they are to lie up.
If one ferret kills a rabbit by itself, it is more likely to

remain in the quiet enjoyment of a meal alone, than when
disturbed by two or three others, all pulling different
directions and fighting together.

Give your ferrets plenty of time, and if one shows up
leave him alone, and do not attempt to pick them up
until they all, or nearly all, show.

Avoid ferrets that are always showing up and running
about above ground; they are as bad as lying hounds. A

FIG. 15.—PICKING UP A FERRET.

ferret to do his work efficiently must keep well out of
sight.

Should your ferrets kill and lie up with a rabbit, and
you are shooting more for sport than extermination, and
consequently want to get on, there are several plans to
be adopted for getting them out. Probably the most
successful is to paunch a warm rabbit, carry the paunch
about to the holes on the windward side, and blow the
fumes in. This seldom fails. Or stamping about with

the feet on top of the earth will sometimes cause them to come out. Or again, you may run a line ferret loosely through the earth, not letting him fix on the rabbit, but frequently pulling him out, when the loose ones will often follow him. Pulling the shot out of a cartridge and discharging it down a hole is not to be recommended. There is not only a chance of accidents, but when the shot is withdrawn the powder does not sometimes force the wadding out of the gun, and consequently the next shot you have, unless you take the precaution of looking down your barrels, you will have a burst gun. Should none of these plans succeed you must either wait and exercise your patience, or dig. One of your ferrets should always be a good liner, and a good line ferret possesses qualifications which are actually detrimental in the others. He need not be fast, but he should be very big, a hob for choice, and a regular butcher and a regular bull-dog. There is nothing much more annoying than having to use a shy or a weak ferret on the line. The shy ferret comes back whenever you pull at him slightly, so that you cannot tell whether he is on a rabbit or not. The weak ferret is not strong enough to kill, and after you have dug two or three yards, and think yourself within reach of your prey, the rabbit, hearing your spade, moves on again. If you want to keep a stock of rabbits from year to year, dig as little as possible. You will probably ferret your earths twice or three times in the season, and if each time you work them you dig, you will in two or three years entirely destroy them.

There is a right way and a wrong way of even picking up a ferret. The wrong way is to put your hand cross-ways of the ferret and pounce down on his neck, when, if you miss him, he will either bite you or shoot back into the earth. The right way, as shown in the two accompanying illustrations, is to pass your hand quietly lengthways over the ferret, your fingers pointing towards the tail, the thumb being on one side of him, the first and second fingers along his back, and the third and fourth fingers on the other side of him. A ferret seldom bites when handled like this, and if he shies back you keep him up to you with the first and second fingers, which are behind his quarters. When advancing to pick up a ferret

FIG. 16—THE RIGHT WAY TO HOLD A FERRET.

be very quiet in all your movements, and never, if possible, put a dead rabbit down to attract a ferret. If you do he will always be looking for it, and there is nothing encourages shying back more than this plan.

A box is better for carrying ferrets about in than a bag. Good ones are to be seen advertised in any maker's catalogue, but the home-made ones, which have struck me as being what is wanted, are semi-circular in shape to fit the hollow of a man's back, with a strap to go over the shoulders, and with two divisions for the ferrets. If you carry ferrets in a bag they get wet from the rain and wet from the ground it is left upon, and if you hang them on a tree the wind blows through and through the bag. All this is avoided by using a box.

The grafts used in digging-out operations should not be too broad or too flat. Six and a half inches across the top, 5in. across the bottom, and 1ft. long is a good size for the iron, while the handle should be about 2ft. 2in. in length. If you have anything broader than this, you move an unnecessary amount of soil. If you have a graft too flat the soil slips off. The best curve is one of about ½in. out of the straight.

CHAPTER VII.

Hints on Shooting to Ferrets.

BY ARTHUR NIBLETT.

THE man who shoots for his liver's sake should not adopt ferreting as a branch of sport; but the man endowed with a sportsman's patience, the quick, smart shot, and the man who likes letting his gun off, should all give it a trial. For my part I find it a pleasing variation, or perhaps a contrast, to the monotony of the day's trudge after outlying cocks, where you think you have had a good day if you have had twelve or fifteen shots. To give an example of what shooting may be got with ferrets when properly worked, I went out with my Scotch keeper one day after lunch; he put seven unmuzzled ferrets into a big place, and then sat on a rail and smoked his pipe. I stood against a tree, and in fourteen minutes had eighteen shots, bagging sixteen rabbits.

If you live on your shoot, and are an idle man, it will be advantageous to try to pick your day. Rabbits bolt best in settled weather, and never bolt better than when there is a set frost, or after a fall of snow when it has started to freeze again. The warm, muggy, summer-like day is unfortunately as bad for ferreting as it is for pike-fishing.

Ferreting is best carried out by one gun and a keeper.

If two men go out for a day's ferreting together, one of them is certain to be disappointed, for one gun will be sure to have the monopoly of the shooting. If you go out with a keeper he need not shoot where one gun can command all the holes.

It is a great thing in ferreting to stand at the right distance from the earth, near enough to make sure of killing your rabbits dead, but not so near as to stop their bolting or as to blow them to pieces. Stand absolutely still and do not fidget. It is more important than not talking. If a rabbit shows his head outside a hole, shoot him; do not wait to give him a run. If you wait to give him this privilege, he will probably go to ground again, when it is three to one he will not bolt a second time. In taking a sitting shot of this description do not bring your gun up to your shoulder as if you were shooting a pigeon out of a trap, as however quick, the rabbit will probably be quicker in disappearing, but raise it very, very slowly. In adopting this plan you are much more likely to get a shot.

Never go to pick up dead rabbits at the mouths of the earth (with the possible exception of a ferret being likely to drag one in) until you have finished. If you wound a rabbit, and there is the slightest chance of his scrambling in, give him a second barrel without hesitation.

In ferreting hedgerows with two guns it is hard to place them so that both can safely take shots over the mouths of the holes. If standing exactly opposite to one another, and at right angles to the fence, they can neither of them shoot with safety; while if they both stand by the side of the fence twenty yards behind the ferrets, they will both have awkward going-away shots, which will probably lead to a lot of crippled rabbits. The best plan is for one gun to stand a gun-shot from the fence at right angles, and the other twenty yards behind the ferrets, by the side of the fence. They will then both be able to shoot with safety. Where there is a deep ditch, the gun that elects to stand by the side of the fence should always be on that side, as he can see to shoot up the ditch, for rabbits are very fond of running a ditch, if a dry one. The prettiest ferreting of all is on a fairly steep, open hill side or bank. In this case, the gun always stands below the earths. Shooting at rabbits on a steep bank is most deceptive, and I have seen really good shots miss many through inability to calculate the rate at which they were travelling.

If you use a retriever at all, he must not only be perfectly broken, but very quick. A dog that has to be shouted at is worse than useless, and a slow, pottering old dog that is either slow in his paces or fumbles with his rabbits had better be left at home. You do not want much nose, or intelligence, but perfect steadiness and quickness when sent and in the return.

CHAPTER VIII.

Diseases.

THE diseases of ferrets are few but they are, as a rule, virulent, and, what is worse, mostly contagious. We have seen how ferrets may be kept healthily; but should disease make its appearance, it is necessary to know how to combat it, because when an outbreak occurs it is so likely to extend through the whole stock; and if one neglects it in the first one attacked the prospects for the remainder are seriously bad. Moreover, there is this to be said, that the great majority of ferret-keepers are quite unacquainted with or incorrectly informed upon the pathology of ferret diseases. It is really difficult to say which state of things is the more unfortunate; the result is, as a rule, identical.

The principal diseases of ferrets are: Distemper (and its many attendant complications), Ear Canker, and Mange, or Scabies. Here it may be stated that in many handbooks purporting to deal with ferret troubles, Footrot is also put down as a specific disease. It is in reality nothing of the sort but merely one phase of the Mange trouble. Much of the information here given is based upon a series of articles which appeared in the columns of "*The Exchange and Mart*" from the pen of that journal's veterinary correspondent.

DISTEMPER.

As in the case of the dog, distemper is due to a filter-passing organism identical in every particular with that causing the disease in dogs, cats, rabbits, and other animals. Further, it is not merely very contagious, but highly fatal in the case of ferrets.

Symptoms.—In its most characteristic form there is a yellowish discharge from the eyelids and nostrils. Though at first watery it gradually thickens and when it dries up closes the eyelids and plugs the nostrils. Frequent sneezing, snoring, and snuffling are accompaniments as a result of breathing difficulties. Later a cough super-venes, and if the disease is progressive the lungs are attacked, and the breathing is distressing, rapid, and perhaps of the pumping kind. Again, pleurisy may develop and with it a moaning noise may accompany each respiratory act. If enteritis occurs, as evidenced by constant vomitings and frequent diarrhœa, with perhaps the fæcal discharges tinged with blood, the patient is in a really bad condition, especially if in addition there are prolapsus of the bowel, disinclination for food, intolerance to light, high and low temperatures alternately, and great emaciation.

Treatment.—Unless the disease is combated at the outset there is not much chance of recovery even if a skilled veterinary surgeon can be consulted and his advice acted upon. Aspirin, in 2½ gr. doses, should be dissolved in fresh milk or sprinkled on a little rabbit or other flesh, and repeated twice or thrice daily. If, too, the weather should be wet and cold sick ferrets must be kept very warm and scrupulously clean. A few drops of equal parts of oil of eucalyptus and beech-wood creosote should be sprinkled on the floor of the sleeping-compartment of the hutch for the occupants to inhale. From time to time, eyelids, nostrils, and lips will need cleaning. For this purpose a 1 per cent. solution of permanganate of potassium will prove effective, especially if the patient be smeared with boracic vaseline. Recovered ferrets need to be watched carefully, as they carry the infection and spread it to others for some time. Before, therefore, allowing them to mix with " clean " ferrets they should be rubbed over with a piece of sponge saturated in one part of " Budge " to seven parts of water. Body, eyes, nostrils, and mouth should all be treated to the dressing.

EAR CANKER (PARASITIC).

As in the dog and also in the cat, the ferret is the subject to parasitic ear canker, the mite being practically identical with that responsible for the trouble in the two animals above named, namely, *Chorioptes auricularum*. With young ferrets especially, it frequently proves fatal, while in adults it is also objectionable and most infectious.

Symptoms.—The parasites referred to set up a virulent form of inflammation of the lining of the ear cavity with the discharge of much serum and wax. Upon this the mites seem to thrive amazingly and to produce much fæcal matter in the form of brownish dirt, which may in severe cases, distend the ear cavity. When this debris appears in the form of a cindery lump or as dust, all the stages may be found commingled. Should the discharges undergo decomposition they aggravate the inflammation, and may become ulcerative in form extending to the bones of the ear and causing meningitis and death.

Besides the dirty condition of the ear cavities and the general irritation there set up, the affected animals in their endeavours to obtain relief by scratching at the root of the ear affected, create a sore. This may develop to such an extent that convulsions may be ultimately set up. These may occur so often that the ferret may become so sleepy as only to wake up to scratch the ear. Gradually in such a case the appetite becomes so poor that from sheer exhaustion, due to want of food, it succumbs, or it may be from meningitis.

Treatment.—For this the following may be recommended: Strong mercurial ointment, 1 dr.; pure carbolic acid, ½ dr.; and olive oil to make 1½ oz. of the whole. The ear to be dressed should be held at the point with the thumb and forefinger of the left hand, and a few drops of the liquid from the well-shaken bottle should be allowed to fall into the cavity. Next the root of the ear should be *gently* manipulated a few times between the thumb and forefinger of the right hand until the liquid has spread over the whole internal lining of the ear down to the drum. Before releasing the ear with the left hand it should be freed as much as possible from the superfluous dressing, using for this operation a piece of cotton-wool; the other ear must then be similarly treated. Repeat the dressing every fourth day for a few times, in order to ensure that no mites are left to recommence the trouble. All ferrets that are affected and living in the same hutch must receive like treatment.

It must be distinctly understood that to free the ferrets from their tormentors and not to use an efficient means for dealing with the hutch would be an act of folly. For this purpose thoroughly scald it with boiling water containing a strong infusion of carbolic, or other known disinfectant. Ferret-breeders must anticipate the probability of young stock, especially in hot weather, showing signs of infestation one to three weeks after birth.

FOOTROT.

This is not a disease in itself but a phase of Mange, or Scabies (which *see*).

MANGE, OR SCABIES.

Ferrets, like dogs, are often the victims of Mange, especially the Sarcoptic form and less often of the Follicular form. Each is due to the presence of a specific mite—*Saroptes scabei hydrochaeri* and *Demodex folliculorum*. The former is highly contagious, the latter is not so. Moreover, Sarcoptic Mange is transmissible alike to man and to certain other animals. Centres of infection are hutches, boxes, or bags (these latter should never be used) which have been employed in transporting mangy specimens, as well as by the introduction of a fresh occupant. Mange may also be introduced by a ferret coming in contact with other of its relations or even with dogs and man. The disease is a highly contagious one and appears on the under-surface of the feet and around the claws. Or, again, it may manifest itself on the body, the skin of which has a moist appearance and gives off a most objectionable odour. The head is also attacked.

A good and safe remedy consists of the application of a gammexane-containing dressing. This should be applied to the whole of the body, and repeated after ten days until all roughness and irritation have disappeared. In addition the animals affected should be kept warm and fed on freshly-killed rabbits, rats, etc., with a plentiful supply of fresh milk. Needless to say hutches should be disinfected as in the case of Ear Canker and renewed at least once a week before the final dressing is applied.

WORMS.

For worms, from which ferrets suffer a good deal, four or five grains of finely-powdered areca nut given in milk on an empty stomach, followed on each occasion half an hour later by five or six drops of castor oil, will prove effective.

CUTS.

For cuts and bad scratches there is nothing so effectual as bathing the parts with a rose-pink solution of permanganate of potash, and afterwards applying boric acid ointment.

TICKS.

Considering the nature of their work in places where the ticks pass the great portion of their lives, it would be surprising if ferrets, like dogs, did not get infested with these blood-sucking parasites, which, when full-fed, fall from their hosts. The first portion of the life of the tick is spent upon grass and other herbage. While a vegetable feeder he is of quite modest dimensions. Once he finds a suitable host—dogs, ferrets, etc.—he quickly assumes aldermanic proportions. On no account should a tick be forcibly pulled from a ferret. A little paraffin and sweet oil (1 part of the former to 8 of the latter) will give the ticks their quietus. Hutches that have housed tick-infested ferrets should be treated to a strong solution of carbolic, or other reliable disinfectant.

FLEAS AND LICE.

Here, again, the ferret resembles the dog, inasmuch as he is troubled with both the above-named objectionable insects. The ferret should first be muzzled, and then carefully sprayed with spirits of camphor, avoiding the head. This will either kill or so stupefy the pests that they may be readily combed away over a vessel of hot water. In the case of lice more than one spraying will be necessary. Oil of Sassafras will also prove a useful and effective insecticide. The paraffin and oil as advised for ticks may be beneficially employed. The sleeping quarters and bedding also need attention.

It should be noted that, as the *Exchange & Mart* has discontinued its editorial supplement, its Expert Advice Service is no longer available.

INDEX.

55

F

Feeding, 15
  courts, 10
  dam, 22
  during gestation, 22
  importance of, 15
  vessels, 6, 7
  working ferrets, 18
  young ferrets, 22
Ferret-courts, 10, 12, 13, 17
  Carr's (Mr. Lascelles) dimensions and plans of, 12, 13
Ferreting rabbits, 25, 45
  from a hedge, 36
  buildings, 50
  corn-ricks, 36
  rats, 27, 35
Fitch, 3
Fitchet, 3
Fleas, 54
Flooring, cinder-and-tar, 13
Food, 15
Foot-rot, 53
Foumart, 3
Frost, effects of, 45
Fumigating lying-up ferrets, 34

G

General management, 15
Gestation, 21
Grafts used in digging-out, 44
Gun, hints on using, 46
Gunners, position of, in ferreting hedges, 46

H

Handling ferrets, 23, 41, 43
Heat, period of, 21
Hedges, ferreting, 36, 56
Hob, 22
Holding, right way of, 43
Hutches, 4
  barrel, 9
  bedding for, 7, 9, 10, 13
  Boulton and Paul's 6
  dimensions of, 6

Hutches—
  for restricted space, 8
  litter for, 13
  makeshifts for, 9
  painting, 7
  self-cleansing, 8
  sleeping compartments of, 6, 7, 10, 11, 12
  Spratt's Patent, 6, 8

I

Insecticide, 7

J

Jills, 10
  treatment of when breeding, 22

L

Lice, 54
Light for ferrets, 19
Line ferret, use of good, 42
  woring on a, 32
Litter, 7, 13
Lost ferrets, recovering, 36
"Lying-up," 27, 29, 32, 33, 41
  remedies for, 34, 42

M

Makeshifts for hutches, 9
Management, general, 15
Mange, 52
Mustelidæ, 1
Muzzle, brass, 40
  indiarubber, 29
  leather, 28, 40
  ring and rod, 28
  string, 32
Muzzling, 30

N

Natural history, 1
New blood, introduction of, 21
Number of ferrets to employ, 40, 45
  of persons to go ferreting, 45

Printed in the United Kingdom
by Lightning Source UK Ltd.
111820UKS00001B/8